S O C C E R
Around the World

Dale E. Howard

CHILDRENS PRESS®

CHICAGO

Dedication
To the children
who play soccer
around the world

Photo Credits
Cover: ©David Cannon/Allsport; Page 1, ©Bill Witt; 4, Shaun Botterill/Allsport;
5, Stock Montage, Inc.; 7, Shaun Botterill/Allsport; 8, ©Tony Quinn/SportsLight;
9, Bob Thomas Sports Photography; 10, David Cannon/Allsport USA; 11, The
Bettmann Archive; 12, North Wind Picture Archives, hand-colored by North Win
13, Shaun Botterill/Allsport; 15, Bob Thomas Sports Photography; 16, ©Joe
Angeles/Root Resources; 18, The Bettmann Archive; 19, Bob Thomas Sports
Photography; 20, SportsChrome East/West; 21, ©Popperfoto; 22, Courtesy Italia
Government Travel Office, USA; 23, 25 (bottom), Bob Thomas Sports
Photography; 25 (top), ©Tony Quinn/SportsLight; 26, Allsport/Pressens Bild; 27,
Bob Thomas Sports Photography; 28, Dave Cannon/Allsport; 29, The Bettmann
Archive; 31, Allsport; 33 ©Tony Quinn/SportsLight; 34, Bob Thomas Sports
Photography; 35, ©Popperfoto; 36, Allsport; 38, Simon Bruty/Allsport USA; 39,
©Cameramann International, Ltd.; 41, ©Tony Quinn/SportsLight; 42 (bottom),
UPI/Bettmann; 42-43 (top), The Bettmann Archive; 44, Stephen Dunn/Allsport;
46, Jed Jacobson/Allsport USA; 47 (all photos), ©Phil Stephens Photography

Editorial Staff
Project Editor: Mark Friedman
Design and Electronic Composition: TJS Design
Photo Editor: Jan Izzo

Library of Congress Cataloging-in-Publication Data
Howard, Dale E.
Soccer around the world / Dale E. Howard.
p. cm.—(World Cup soccer) Includes index.
ISBN 0-516-08046-6
1. World Cup (Soccer)—Juvenile literature. [1. World Cup (Soccer)—History.
2. Soccer—History.] I. Title. II. Series

GV943.49.H69 1994   93-485
796.334'668—dc20   (

Table of Contents

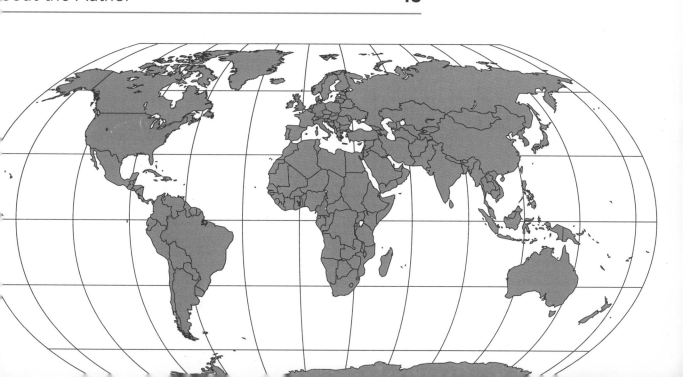

A Brief History of Soccer

Put a ball in front of a child, and he or she will probably try to kick it. It just seems natural. S it seems that people have played with balls from the beginning of time.

In ancient China, jugglers worked with wick er balls made out of bamboo twigs woven together. Today's best soccer players can also juggle a ball with their feet, keeping it in the air for long periods of time.

Tsu chu was an ancient Chinese game played b two teams with a stuffed leather ball. The object of the game was to kick the ball into a goal, just like modern soccer. Teams celebrated the emperor birthday by playing *tsu chu*.

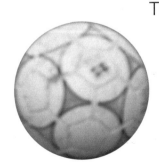

The ancient Japanese also playe a team game by moving a bal up and down a field, trying to put the ball into a goal. The Japanese called the game *kemari.* It's possible that the Japanese and Chinese played the game against each other about 50 B.C.

Native Americans in Mexico and Central America also played ball games. In most of these games, players were not allowed to touch the ball with their hands. That's just like soccer as we play it!

An early Chinese foot game

The Greeks and then the Romans played a game in which they could use their hands to move a ball. The Greeks called it *episkyros*. The Romans called it *harpastum* and probably played it in England, a land they conquered.

Modern soccer developed over several centuries in England. It is possible that soccer came from the Roman game *harpastum*. But we also know that the ancient Irish and English peoples played a ball game too. Perhaps the two games were mixed together.

In their world travels, English explorers, soldiers, settlers, traders, and tourists took along their beloved soccer. They introduced the game to people everywhere, and the game gained popularity on every continent.

By 1900 soccer teams from different countries were playing against each other. They needed to agree on a single set of rules. On May 21, 1904, the *Fédération Internationale de Football Association*, or FIFA, was formed by representatives from France, Belgium, Holland, Denmark, Sweden, Switzerland, and Spain. England joined the FIFA a year later. In the next years, more and more countries joined. Today the FIFA rules international soccer. It is responsible for holding the World Cup every four years.

The World's Game

The World Cup is soccer's world championship tournament. After playing early elimination rounds, 24 teams representing different countries qualify for the final championship tournament. Two teams automatically qualify for the championship tournament—the reigning World Cup champion and the current year's host country.

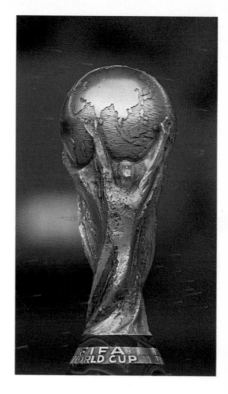

The World Cup trophy

In 1994, the United States hosted the World Cup championship tournament for the first time. Games were played in several U.S. cities, with the championship match between Brazil and Italy held at the Rose Bowl in Pasadena, California. Brazil won, becoming the first four-time World Cup winner.

The festive scene at a soccer
match in Trinidad

The 1990 World Cup was watched by more than a billion people living on al six continents. With the 1994 World Cup in the United States, the audience grew even larger.

Soccer has surely become the world's most popular sport. In more than 175 countries, soccer is the major national sport.

More than 2 million players are registered with official soccer organizations, and about 275,000 clubs play in official leagues and tournaments.

The real reason soccer is the world's game is that s many people love it. Children play soccer in village streets and city parks all over Africa, Asia, and Central and South America. Junior leagues play throughout Europe and North America. Girls' and men's soccer is gaining popularity in schools and lleges. And in virtually every U.S. city and town, untless kids love playing organized soccer.

ccer fans like to dress up in their favorite team's ors to attend games. Pride in their city is bound with pride in the local soccer team. When it mes to international competition (like the World p) people feel the ne way about their ccer team as they do out their country. thing else, except ssibly the Olympic mes, carries so much triotic emotion.

any international tch, you will find usands of fans dressed in their team's colors and ving their national flags. Soccer is truly the rld's game.

Enthusiastic Brazilian soccer fans

England

Soccer began in England. A legend tells of a game played against the Roman conquerors in the town of Derby, in A.D. 217.

Colors
White shirts, royal blue shorts, white socks

World Cup Champions
1966

1994 World Cup
Failed to qualify for the final tournament of 24 countries

Despite the legend, we aren't sure if soccer comes from the Roman ball game *harpastum*, or from an ancient Irish ball game, or a combination of the two. We do know that a ball game has been hugely popular in England for at least the past thousand years.

Early ball games were played in country lanes and village streets. Sometimes goals were miles apart. Sometimes goals were at either end of a town's main street. Players moved the ball in any way they could. The games were like mob riots.

These games grew so rowdy and violent that many English rulers tried to outlaw them. But it didn't work.

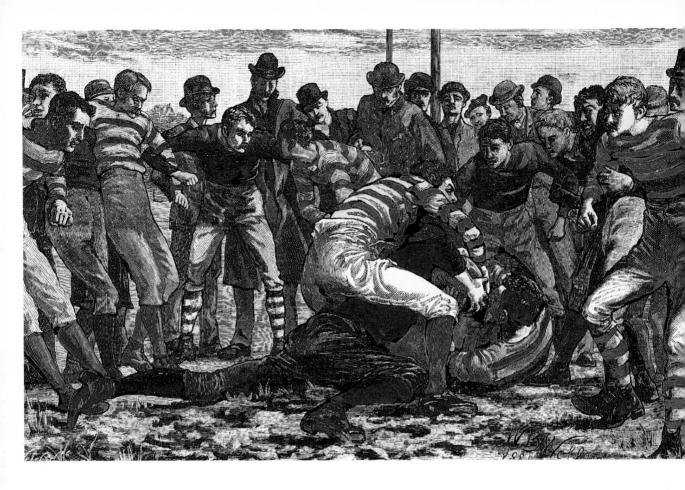

Early English soccer was an extremely rough game.

People continued to play soccer. The English simply love the game.

By the 1800s students at English schools and universities played the game. Each school made up its own rules. In the 1850s many clubs were also formed to play the game, each with its own rules.

Some clubs allowed players to use their hands, and others did not. Some allowed players to kick each other's shins. They called this hacking.

inally, in 1863, the game split into two games,
ugby and soccer. You could use your hands to
dvance the ball in rugby. In soccer, you could not.
Rugby gave rise to American, Canadian, and
ustralian football. Soccer became popular in the
st of the world.)

On October 26, 1863,
ourteen schools and
lubs met to decide on
ne set of rules. From
his meeting, the Football
ssociation was formed.
he F.A. is the oldest
occer organization in the
orld. In fact, its name
association," shortened
o "assoc," was the root
or the word "soccer."

Action from the 1992 F.A. Cup,
which is played at London's
Wembley Stadium every year

t that time, England had colonies all over
he world. When the English traveled to other

countries, they taught people how to play soccer. The game was soon being played everywhere. By 1900, teams from different countries were playing against each other.

England has perhaps the best soccer leagues in th world. Students at schools and universities continu to play the game. English professional clubs also play for the European Cup against the best pro- fessional teams from all over Europe.

Until the 1950s, England was considered the best soccer-playing country in the world. But in the 195 World Cup, they were shocked by a 1-0 loss to the United States. Things got worse for England. In 1953, the Hungarian national team defeated them 6-3 at Wembley Stadium. It was the first time England had ever lost a soccer game at home to a foreign team. In the 1954 World Cup, Uruguay bea them. In the 1958 Cup tournament, they lost a pla off game to Russia. And in 1962, Brazil defeated them. These defeats led people to think that the

English weren't very good at the game they originated.

In the 1960s, England rebuilt its national team under manager Alf Ramsey. He assembled a powerful team with great stars such as captain Bobby Moore, record scorer Bobby Charlton, and the thrilling goalkeeper Gordon Banks. With this great team, England won the 1966 World Cup.

England's Geoff Hurst scores his third goal in the 1966 World Cup championship game.

England's World Cup success was short-lived. It failed to qualify or get past the quarterfinals in World Cup play until 1990. That year England finished fourth, playing perhaps the best soccer of any country in the final tournament. But England has again fallen on hard times—it failed to qualify for the 1994 World Cup tournament.

Germany

Germany defeated Argentina 1-0 to win the 1990 World Cup. But Germany could not repeat its championship in the next tournament, as it lost to Bulgaria in the 1994 World Cup quarterfinals.

Colors
White shirts, black shorts,
white socks

World Cup Champions
1954, 1974, 1990

1994 World Cup
Lost to Bulgaria in quarterfinals

ermany has one of the best World Cup
records. It has reached the championship
me six times and won three of them. Besides the
90 win, Germany beat Holland in 1974 and upset
ungary 3-2 to win the 1954 Cup. That Hungarian
am, led by the great Ferenc Puskás, had been
defeated for four years and was considered one
the best teams of all time.

ccer came to Germany in 1876, when England's
otball Association rules were translated into
erman. The game grew slowly in Germany. Some
ermans disliked it because it was "the English
me." But others loved the game and didn't care
here it came from. Finally, in the late 1950s,
ccer had become a national passion.

ermany now has a powerful national team
cause of its strong professional league—the
deral League, or *Bundeslige*. Although it is only
few decades old, the *Bundeslige* has sent more
ams to European club championships than any

untry in Europe. One of these teams, Bayern
unich, won the European Cup three times in a
w, from 1974 to 1976.

anz Beckenbauer led Bayern Munich to those
ee straight European Cup wins, and he was also
e star of the 1974 World Cup championship team.
at team consisted of six players from Bayern
unich and others who played together on profes-
nal clubs. Because these players were familiar
th each other, they were able to develop quickly
o an incredible passing and attacking machine.

ermany has continued to field strong national
ams. They reached the World Cup championship
me in 1982, 1986, and 1990. Although they were
minated in the 1994 Cup quarterfinals, Germany
still one of the world's top soccer teams.

Andreas Brehme holds the
World Cup trophy. He scored
the winning goal in the 1990
championship game.

many and Uruguay met in
1928 Olympics.

Italy

Colors
Blue shirts, white shorts,
blue socks

World Cup Champions
1934, 1938, 1982

1994 World Cup
Lost championship game
to Brazil

Italy has long been a dominant team in world socce
Through the years, it has been a major force in
both the World Cup and the Olympics.

The Italians celebrate their 1936 Olympic gold medal in soccer. The games were held in Berlin, Germany.

Italy has won three World Cups and finished second once. Italy probably had the best team in the world in the 1930s, when it won not only the 1934 and 1938 World Cups, but also the 1936 Olympic Games gold medal. At that time the Italian government supported the team. It felt that the soccer team showed the world how strong Italy was in all parts of life.

Since the 1950s, Italy has produced some of the world's strongest professional clubs. They provide good training and practice to players who then join the national team. Teams from the city of Milan won four European Cups in the 1960s.

Some people believe that soccer developed from the Roman game *harpastum*. If that's true, Italians played a form of soccer 2,000 years ago!

The ancient Italian game *calcio* is played for 1990s fans at a festival in Florence, Italy.

Italians in Florence did play a form of kickball from the 14th to 16th centuries. This game, called *calcio*, allows players to use their hands to throw the ball over a goal line. It resembles American football and is still played for tourists during a yearly festival. Soccer as we know it came to Italy from England in 1887. Major cities like Turin, Genoa, and Milan soon had soccer clubs.

Italy began international play in 1910—and didn't do very well. It was then that Vittorio Pozzo took over Italian soccer. Vittorio introduced a new, attacking style of play, and Italy became a world soccer power. From 1930 to 1940, Italy lost only seven out of the 67 international games it played.

Then in the late 1940s, Italy changed its style of play again. Instead of attacking the opponent's bal, players focused most of their time and energy

n defending their own goal. But this defensive

yle did not lead to much international success.

y 1982, Italy had moved
ack to an offense-
iented game and
efeated Germany in
e World Cup champi-
nship game. Italy had
ecome only the second
am in history to win
ree World Cups.

aly returned to the
orld Cup champion-
ip game in 1994. After

Coach Vittorio Pozzo is lifted into the air by his players after winning the 1934 World Cup.

attling Brazil to a 0-0 overtime tie, the game

ent to a penalty-kick shootout. Italy lost the Cup

hen its star player, Roberto Baggio, missed his

st penalty kick.

Brazil

Colors
Yellow shirts, blue shorts,
white socks

World Cup Champions
1958, 1962, 1970, 1994

1994 World Cup
Defeated Italy in
championship game

Playing soccer is part of the Brazilian way of life, much like dancing the samba. *The* samba *is a Brazilian dance with a shifting beat. It is often danced by groups of people in a circle.*

Many sports fans say that Brazilians play socc like they dance the *samba*. They seem to play together as if they are all following the same beat. In fact, teams often prepare for a big game by tapping out *samba* rhythms in the team bus. As they warm up for games, Brazilian players often talk and laugh in a circle while juggli and passing a soccer ball back and forth to each other. Juggling the ball like this is difficult, but the Brazilians do it just for fur as if it's second nature.

From children playing soccer in the streets to the 220,000 fans who can pack the Maracanã Stadium in Rio de Janeiro, Brazilians feel that soc-cer is part of their lives. They love their soccer sta

veryone in Brazil knows them by a single nick-
ame. Among Brazilian stars of the past are Didi,
ito, Vava, Jairzinho, Junior, and of course Pelé.

elé actually doesn't know what his name means or
hy people began calling him that. It's just his soc-
er nickname. His family calls him Dico, and his real
ame is Edson Arantes do Nascimento.

220,000 exuberant fans regularly
fill Maracanã Stadium in Rio de
Janeiro, Brazil.

razil is the only country to qualify for every World

Pelé (second from right) amazed the soccer world with his performance in the 1958 World Cup.

Cup finals tournament. It is also the first country to win the World Cup four times (Italy and Germany have won the Cup three times each).

Brazil dominated the 1958 World Cup when Pelé was still a young star. In the '58 quarterfinal game, Pelé scored the only goal in Brazil's 1-0 win over Wales. He then scored three goals when Brazil beat France 5-2 in the semifinals. And in the championship game, Pelé had two more goals in a 5-2 victory over Sweden. Add it up, and Pelé scored six of Brazil's 11 goals in the final three games! Pelé had proven himself the world's best player.

In 1962, the world awaited Pelé's return to the World Cup. But he was injured early in the tournament and missed Brazil's last four games.

is teammates didn't quit, however, and they won
eir second straight Cup. In 1970, Pelé and Brazil
ominated Cup play so throughly that they did not
se or tie a single game in the tournament! Brazil
efeated Italy to become the first ever three-time
up champions.

1994, Brazil met Italy again in the World Cup

ampionship game.

t the end of overtime,

ot a single goal had
cored. In the first

enalty-kick shootout

a Cup championship
ame, Brazil outshot

aly 3-2 to take home

eir unprecedented

ourth World Cup.

Brazil defeated Italy in 1970
for its third World Cup
championship.

Argentina

Colors
Blue and white striped shirts,
black shorts, white socks

World Cup Champions
1978, 1986

1994 World Cup
Lost in second round
to Romania

Argentina lost the first World Cup championship game, in 1930, to Uruguay. It lost the 1990 championship game to Germany. In between, Argentina won the World Cup twice.

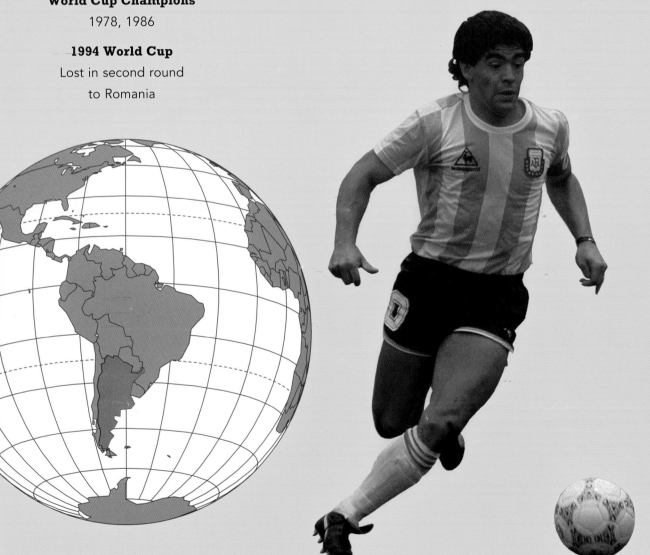

Soccer was first played in Argentina by English sailors and railroad workers. Others were soon playing the game, and Argentina became the second country in the world (after England) to form a soccer league.

The rest of South America learned soccer from Argentine and English players. In 1905, Argentina played its first international match, against Uruguay. This game, played for the Lipton Cup, began one of the oldest international rivalries in soccer. Argentina and Uruguay have played for the Lipton Cup in many years since. (And yes, the Lipton Cup *is* named after the man whose name is on the tea bags! Sir Thomas Johnstone Lipton

Argentina and Uruguay clashed in the 1928 Olympics.

donated the original trophy cup that the winning team took home.)

In 1916, Argentina helped form the South America league and championship with Brazil, Uruguay, and Chile. Argentina didn't win the championship until five years later. Since then, however, it has dominated the league, which now includes most South American countries.

The level of competition between Argentina's soccer clubs is extremely high. Many of the great players from these teams are lured to play in Europe. The European teams offer them much more money than the Argentine teams can afford. Alfredo di Stefano, for example, left Argentina to play for the Spanish club Real Madrid. He also played for Spain's national team. The superstar Diego Maradona has spent most of his professional life playing for Italian teams. But Maradona always plays for Argentina in international competition.

Argentina has appeared in three of the past four World Cup finals. In 1978, it was the host country and won its first championship in its home stadium. Its second championship (1986) was known as "Maradona's Cup." That's because Maradona was so dominant. Argentina won both their quarterfinal and semifinal matches by scores of 2-0... and Maradona scored all the goals *in both games!* When the final game with Germany was tied 2-2, Maradona set up the winning goal with a spectacular pass.

Argentina reached the finals again in 1990, but this time Germany won, 1-0. You can't miss Argentina during World Cup matches. Their blue-and-white striped shirts are famous all over the world. So is their tough, determined style of play.

The 1986 World Cup is called "Maradona's Cup" because Argentina's star player, Diego Maradona (above), was so dominant.

Uruguay

Colors
Light blue shirts, black shorts,
black socks

World Cup Champions
1930, 1950

1994 World Cup
Failed to qualify

Uruguay won the first World Cup ever, beating its oldest rival, Argentina. It did not enter the next two World Cup competitions because of political conflicts. When it did compete again, Uruguay won the Cup in 1950.

Uruguay began playing soccer a little over a century ago, shortly after Argentina took up the game. Like Argentines, Uruguayans learned the game from English sailors and workers. The English and Uruguayans formed soccer clubs and then a league. Two of those early teams are still in existence—Peñarol and Nacional.

From 1923 through its 1930 World Cup victory, Uruguay had the best soccer team in the world. It won the soccer gold medal in both the 1924 and 1928 Olympic Games in Paris and Amsterdam. These victories showed the world that South Americans played soccer just as well as Europeans did.

Devoted Uruguayan fans at a soccer match

lost of the success of this Uruguayan team came om its midfielders. They became known as *la ostilla metallica*, or "the iron curtain." They rarely t opposing players move the ball past them.

the 1950 World Cup, Uruguay reached the finals ithout much trouble. In the championship game ey faced Brazil, the host country. A record crowd f 199,854 spectators packed into Maracanã

The Uruguayans, in their familiar blue jerseys, are consistent contenders in the World Cup tournament.

tadium in Rio de Janeiro

watch the final game.

razil was favored to win,

nd to the delight of the

ome fans, Brazil scored

he first goal.

ruguay then began to

lay with great determination. Juan "Pepe"

chiaffino, the Uruguayan star, took a pass in front of

he Brazilian goal and scored to tie the game. Just

1 minutes before the end of the game, Pepe made

great pass to a teammate for a goal, and the win.

ruguay had beaten their South American rivals in

eir own stadium. The Brazilian crowd was so

unned that people actually fainted in the stands.

ince 1950 Uruguay has failed to advance beyond

e semifinal game, which it reached in 1954 and

970. Still, Uruguay has the sixth-best record in

e World Cup.

Goalkeeper Maspoli dives to save a goal in Uruguay's thrilling 1950 World Cup victory.

Cameroon

Germany ruled Cameroon in the early 1900s, and introduced soccer to the Cameroon people. After World War I, Cameroon was ruled by the French government. The French were also soccer players. People in Cameroon have played soccer for many generations.

Colors
Green shirts, red shorts, yellow socks

Best World Cup Finish
Quarterfinals, 1990

1994 World Cup
Eliminated in first round

Cameroon began its international soccer success in 1964 when one of its teams won the first African Champions' Cup. Another Cameroon team took the Cup in 1971. Since then Cameroon clubs have been among the best in Africa.

Cameroon made its first World Cup appearance in 1982. It was unbeaten…but it also failed to win a game. The truth is that Cameroon tied its three games against Peru, Poland, and Italy. Gaining a tie against Italy was impressive, for Italy went on to win the Cup that year.

In 1990, Cameroon stunned the world by beating defending champion Argentina in the first round of World Cup play. It advanced to the quarterfinal round by beating Rumania and Colombia. Its 3-2 overtime loss to England showed people that Cameroon had become a world soccer power.

Other African countries that joined Cameroon in the 1994 World Cup finals were Nigeria and Morocco.

Republic of (South) Korea

Colors
Red shirts, red shorts, red socks

Best World Cup Finish
First Round, 1954, 1986, 1990, 1994

1994 World Cup
Eliminated in first round

South Korea is one of the strongest soccer teams in Asia. In fact, it is one of the few Asian teams from the Far East ever to qualify for the World Cup final tournament. The other Asian teams to qualify have been from the Middle East, including Iran, Iraq, Kuwait, and Egypt. From the Far East, only the former Dutch East Indies and North Korea have made it.

In 1954, South Korea qualified for its first World Cup final tournament. Although it didn't make it past the first round, it gained experience in world-class soccer. It built on that experience to win the first two Asian Cups in 1956 and 1960.

Soccer is so popular in South Korea that these factory workers are playing on their lunch break.

South Korea returned to the World Cup final tournament in 1986, 1990, and 1994. It didn't make it past the first round, however, but it continues to prove itself the dominant Asian soccer team.

Soccer is played high up in the Himalayan Mountains of Nepal; in the jungles of Indonesia, Burma, and Thailand; in the bustling cities of Hong Kong and Tokyo; and by barefooted children in India's street bazaars. So when the South Koreans take the field in their striking red uniforms, they are representing millions of Asian soccer players.

United States

Colors
White shirts, blue shorts,
red socks

Best World Cup Finish
Semifinals, 1930

1994 World Cup
Lost to Brazil in second round

The United States has entered every World Cup competition. Most of the time, however, the U.S. fails to qualify for the final tournament. In fact, it has made the finals only four times (1930, 1934, 1950, and 1990). Because it was the host country in 1994, it automatically qualified for the final tournament of 24 teams.

English settlers brought the rough and rowdy ball game across the Atlantic centuries ago. We know that colonists in Jamestown played it in 1609. Many early American towns, like Boston in 1657, banned it. As in England, however, the bans did not hold.

Soccer's wide popularity in the United States began in colleges and universities. On November 6, 1869, Princeton and Rutgers played the first college "football" game in America. This was a soccer game, and Rutgers won it 6-4 after four hours of play. These universities

ventually formed a football association with other
y League colleges. The game they were playing
as an early form of soccer.

t the same time, however, Harvard College began
laying rugby, in which players could use their
ands. Other schools joined Harvard. The game

Harvard rugby, early 1900s

they played grew into American football. Football soon became the favorite game among colleges, taking soccer's place.

While college and professional American football grew in popularity, soccer remained rooted in citie with large immigrant populations. In the early 1900s, millions of immigrants came to America from Germany, Italy, Ireland, and other European countries. They played soccer on city streets and playgrounds. City leagues were formed. But socce

An 1856 soccer game among Harvard students

...ill failed to capture national attention.

...he United States Soccer Association joined
...he FIFA in 1913. When the first World Cup
...ournament was held in 1930, the U.S. did quite
...ell. It impressed the world by beating Belgium
...nd Paraguay, then fell to Argentina 6-1 in the
...emifinals.

...he greatest U.S. World Cup win came in 1950.
...veryone thought England had the greatest soccer

1994 U.S. national team goalkeeper Tony Meola

team in the world. The English coach was so su[re] he would win his match with the Americans that he rested Stanley Matthews, his star playe[r]. It was a big mistake. Although England had many shots on the American goal, nothing went in. When the U.S. scored the winning goal[,] the amazed Brazilian crowd rushed the field and carried the America[n] players on their shoulde[rs] as heroes.

1950 was the last World Cup highlight for the U.S. until it hosted the tournament in 1994.

s the host country, the U.S. automatically qualified
or the Cup finals, but nobody gave the Americans
much of a chance to advance. When the U.S. team
upset Colombia in the first round, however, they
id advance to the second round. There, they
rew the eventual champions, Brazil, and lost 1-0.
Nevertheless, the U.S. team's tough play impressed
millions of fans around the world.

Several professional leagues have played in the
U.S. Most have failed. The most successful league
was the North American Soccer League (NASL) in
the 1960s and 70s. Most NASL players were aging
foreign stars such as German sweeper Franz
Beckenbauer, Irish wizard George Best, African
great Eusebio, and England's Gordon Banks. And
Americans were especially thrilled when Pelé
came out of retirement to play for the New
York Cosmos.

Still, American fans preferred baseball, basketball,
and American football. The NASL couldn't compete
with these sports, and it went out of business.

From elementary school to high
school and college, soccer has
become a popular sport among
girls and women of all ages.

More and more young people in the United States are playing soccer just for fun. In fact, more American kids play organized soccer than any other sport, except maybe basketball. The United States Youth Soccer Association sends teams overseas to compete with young players from other countries.

Many people hope that with the success of the 1994 World Cup in the U.S., even more young people will want to play the world's game.

Index

Page numbers in **bold-face type** indicate photos or illustrations.

About the Author

Dale Howard was born and raised in India, where his parents served as missionaries. His love of soccer began in school, when he played center forward and won his school's Best All-Around Athlete award.

After working for twenty years at Open Court Publishing in language arts and curriculum development, he is now managing editor at Meadowbrook Press in Minnesota. He also recently received his Master of Divinity degree from Lutheran Northwestern Theological Seminary in St. Paul, Minnesota.

Mr. Howard is married and has four children.